LOOK OUT, GENTRY!

Written by Elizabeth Moerschel
Illustrated by Eve Funnell

✼This book is based upon real places, animals and events. The characters are alive and well on the beautiful prairie in North Dakota.

Published by Orange Hat Publishing 2018

ISBN 978-1-948365-15-4

Copyrighted © 2018 by Elizabeth Moerschel
All Rights Reserved
Look Out, Gentry!
Written by Elizabeth Moerschel
Illustrated by Eve Funnell

This publication and all contents within may not be reproduced or transmitted in any part or in its entirety without the written permission of the author.

www.orangehatpublishing.com

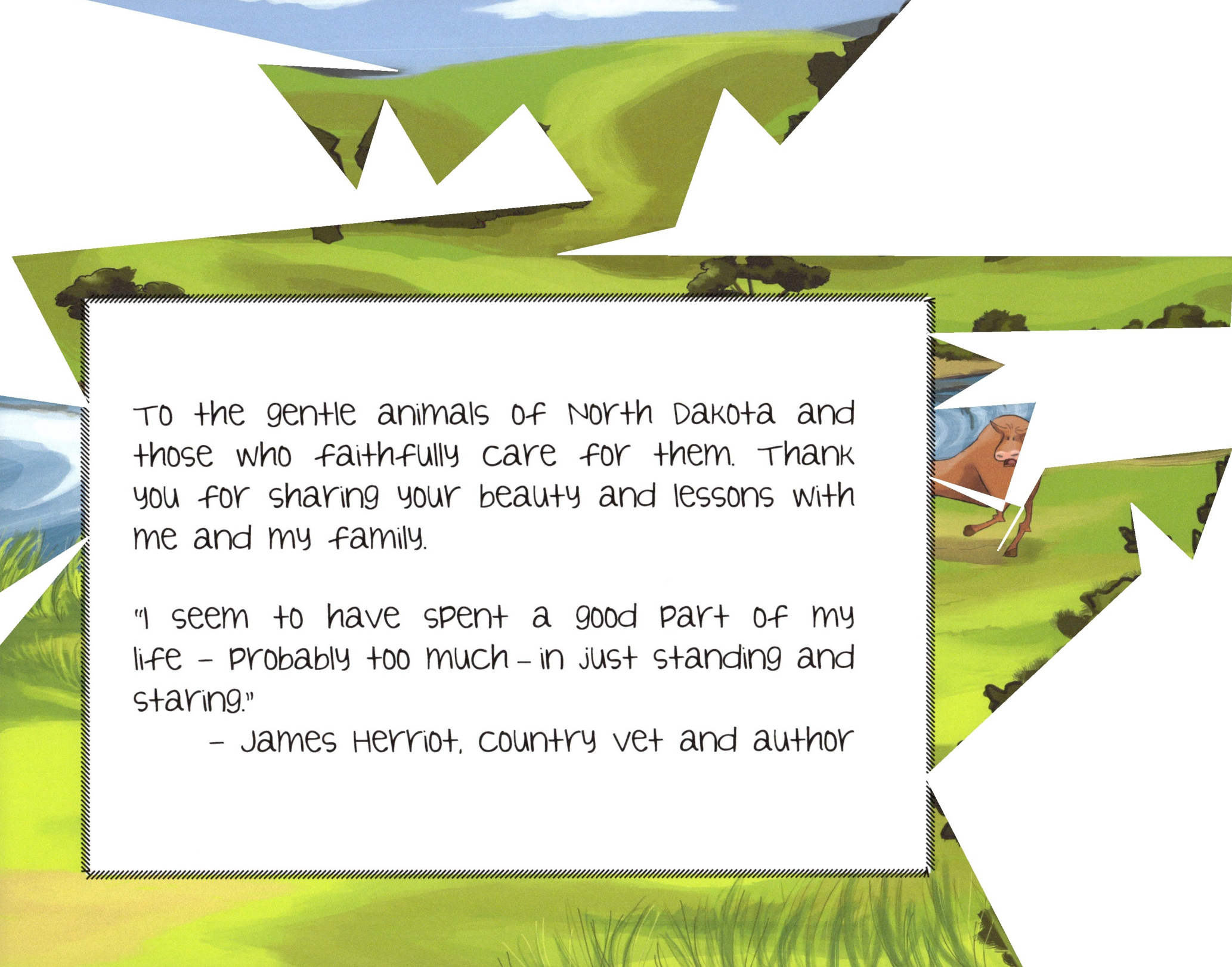

To the gentle animals of North Dakota and those who faithfully care for them. Thank you for sharing your beauty and lessons with me and my family.

"I seem to have spent a good part of my life – probably too much – in just standing and staring."

— James Herriot, country vet and author

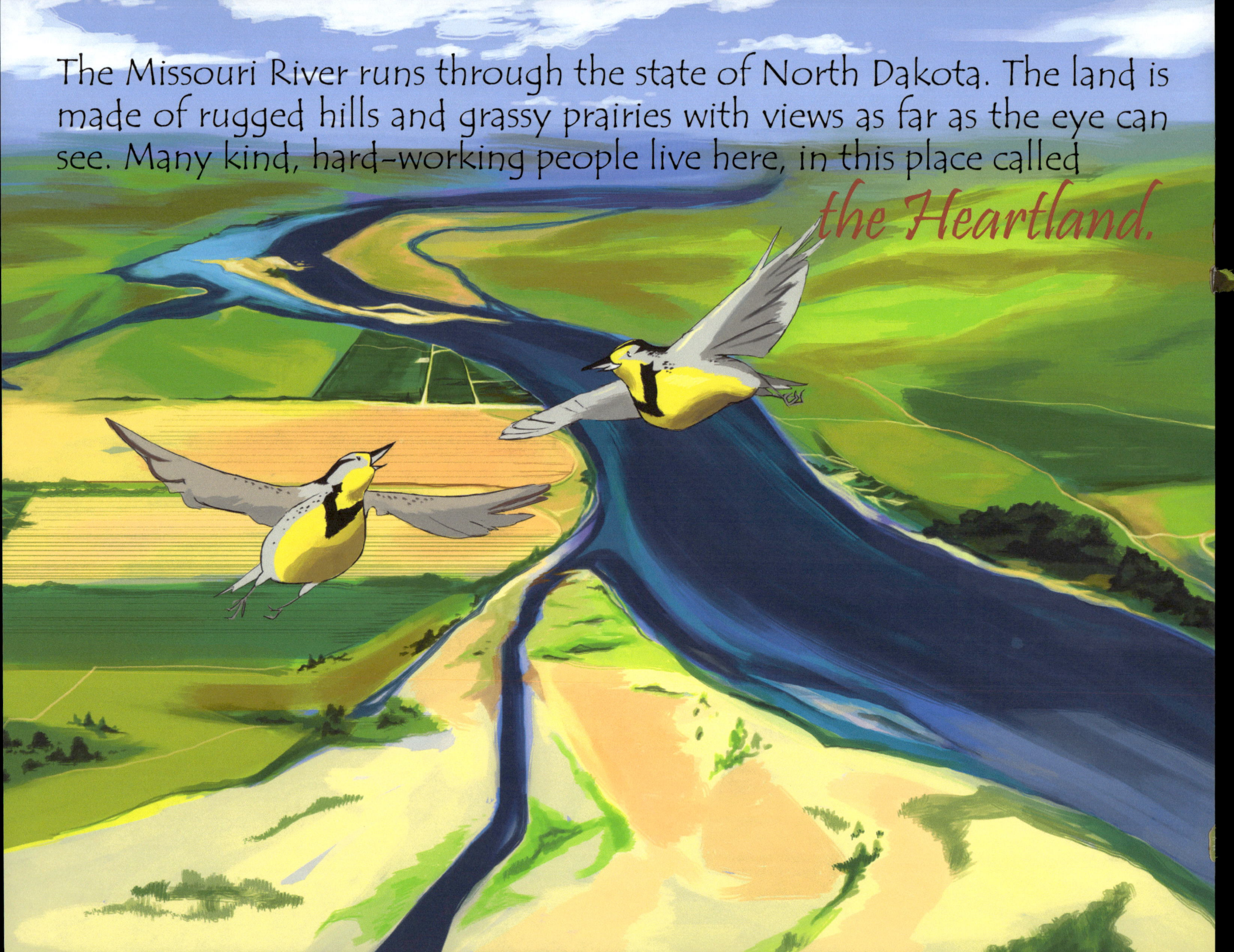

The Missouri River runs through the state of North Dakota. The land is made of rugged hills and grassy prairies with views as far as the eye can see. Many kind, hard-working people live here, in this place called *the Heartland.*

Rancher Dave and his wife, Kathy, live and work here. Their days are filled with many chores like growing crops, cutting hay, mending fences, and raising cattle. The days pass in much the same way, but every now and then something unusual happens…

Meet Gentry, one of Rancher Dave's bulls. Gentry weighs almost 2,000 pounds and lives in a large pen near Rancher Dave's house. Gentry's days also pass in much the same way. He eats hay, takes long naps, and visits with the other animals on the ranch. But sometimes Gentry gets very bored…

Gentry ran away from home, sure that adventure was out there somewhere! As he traveled, he met a busy **black dog** digging a hole. Hoping he had found adventure, he asked, "Is there something exciting in there?" The dog replied, "I am working hard to bury my new bone. You may help if you wish." Gentry was disappointed because burying bones was not exciting for a bull.

Gentry moved along and met two dependable donkeys. The donkeys stood in the long, green grass watching the cows and their calves. Still hoping for adventure, Gentry eagerly asked the donkeys, "Do you know of anything exciting to do?" The donkeys replied, "Well, we are busy protecting the cows. You may help if you wish."

Gentry's heart sank since he did not find watching cows exciting.

Gentry trudged on, still determined to FIND ADVENTURE.

After all, he didn't break out of his pen for nothing! Gentry came upon a gentle gray mare and her frisky foal. The foal was trotting and prancing in circles around the mare. Gentry asked him, "Why are you moving this way and that?" The foal answered, "I am learning how to be strong and fast. You may help if you wish." Gentry was already strong and fast, so helping the foal was definitely not exciting.

Gentry was frustrated! Where was all of the adventure?!?

Rancher Dave came home and saw that Gentry had ESCAPED. He whistled for his clever cattle dog, mounted his horse, and off they went across the hills. Soon, they spotted Gentry off in the distance toward the river. The cattle dog raced ahead.

Gentry saw the cattle dog speeding toward him. He knew he was in trouble for leaving his pen, but was not yet ready to go home. Gentry still wanted to find excitement and adventure. He knew he had to get away from the cattle dog,

SO GENTRY TOOK OFF!

The chase was on! Gentry ran as fast as his hooves could go. The cattle dog was fast, but so was Gentry! Both bull and dog ran through a tall cornfield…

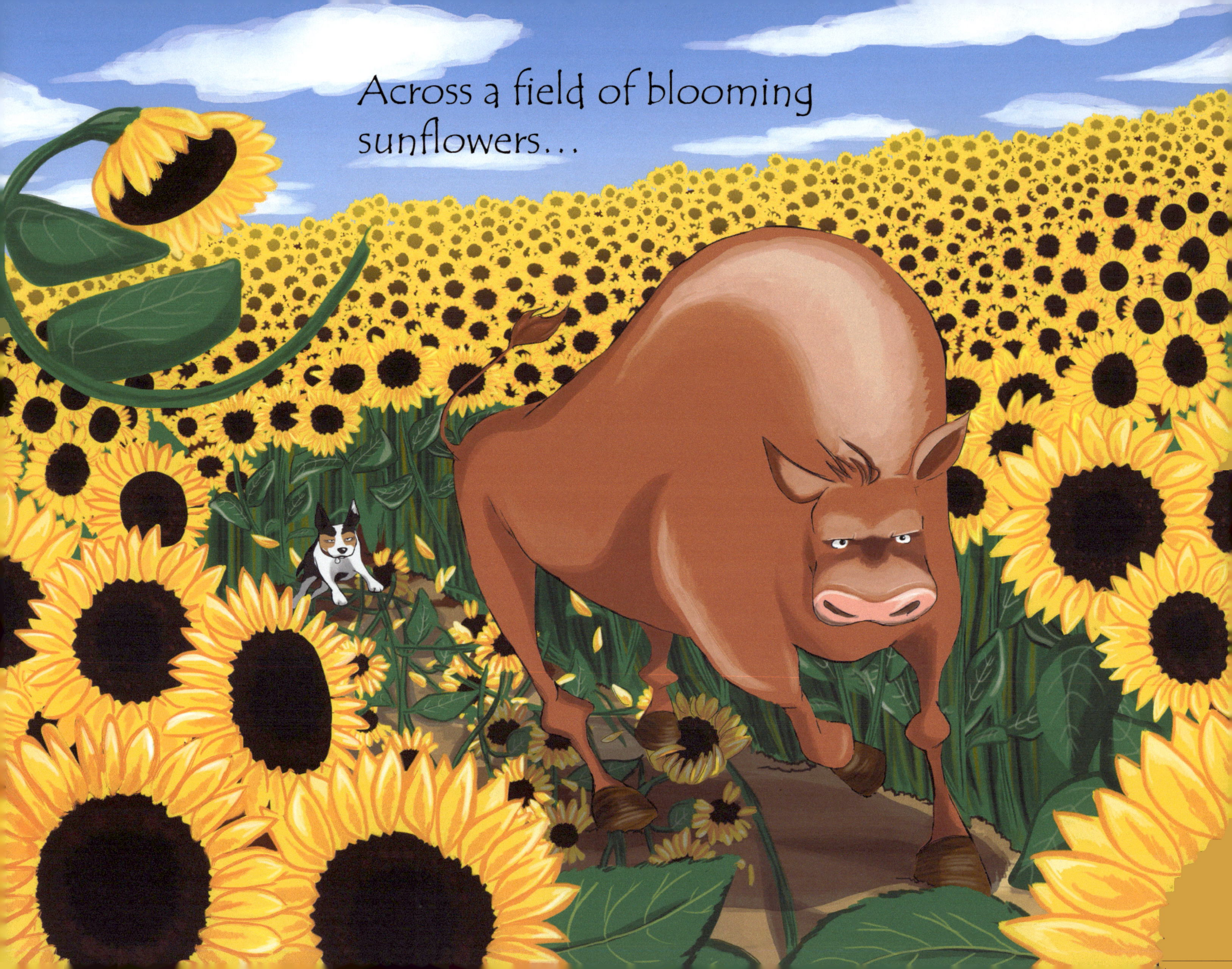
Across a field of blooming sunflowers…

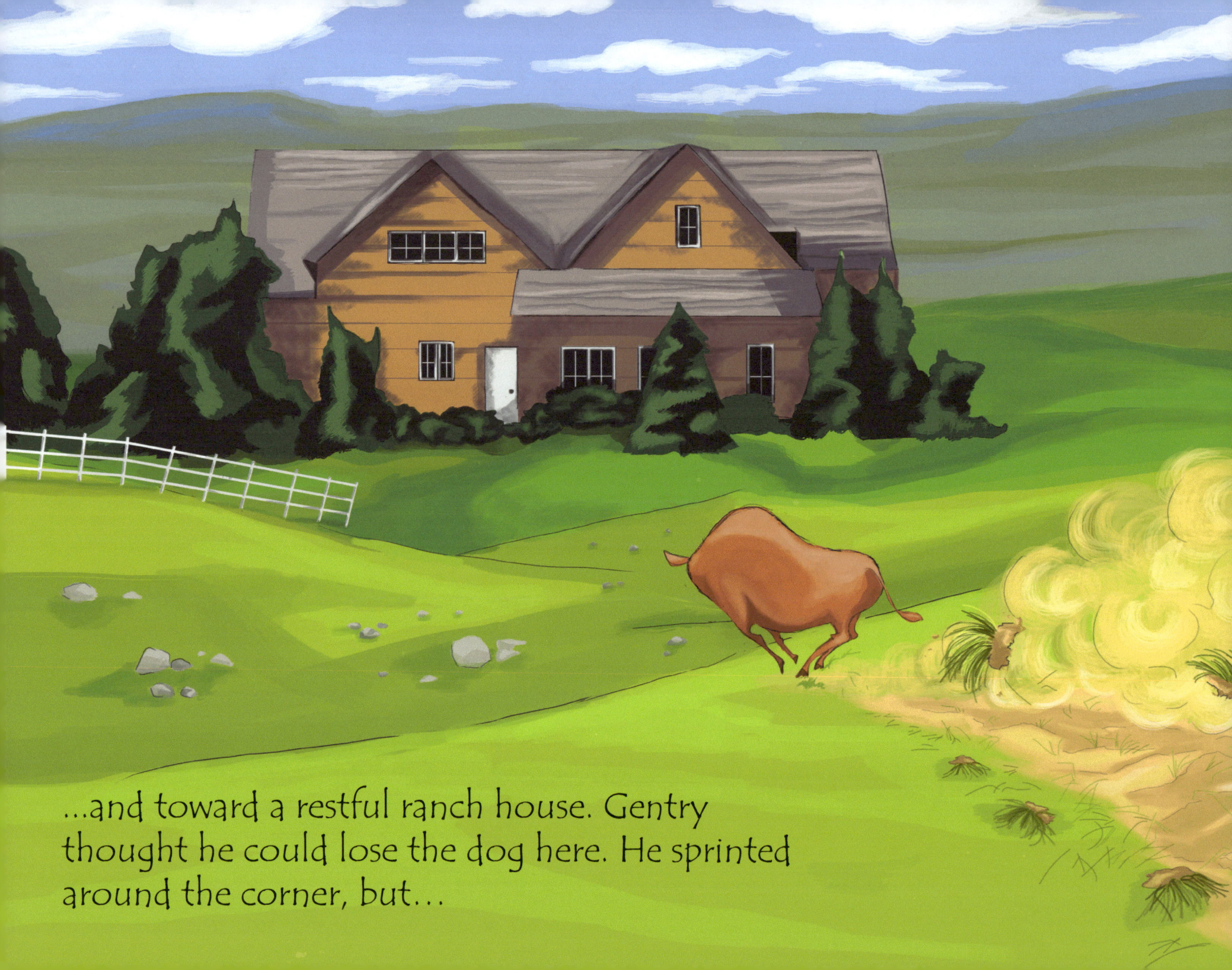

...and toward a restful ranch house. Gentry thought he could lose the dog here. He sprinted around the corner, but...

SPLASH!

Gentry found himself in the deep end of a swimming pool. The pool was covered, but Gentry, being such a big bull, tore right through the cover, and in he went!

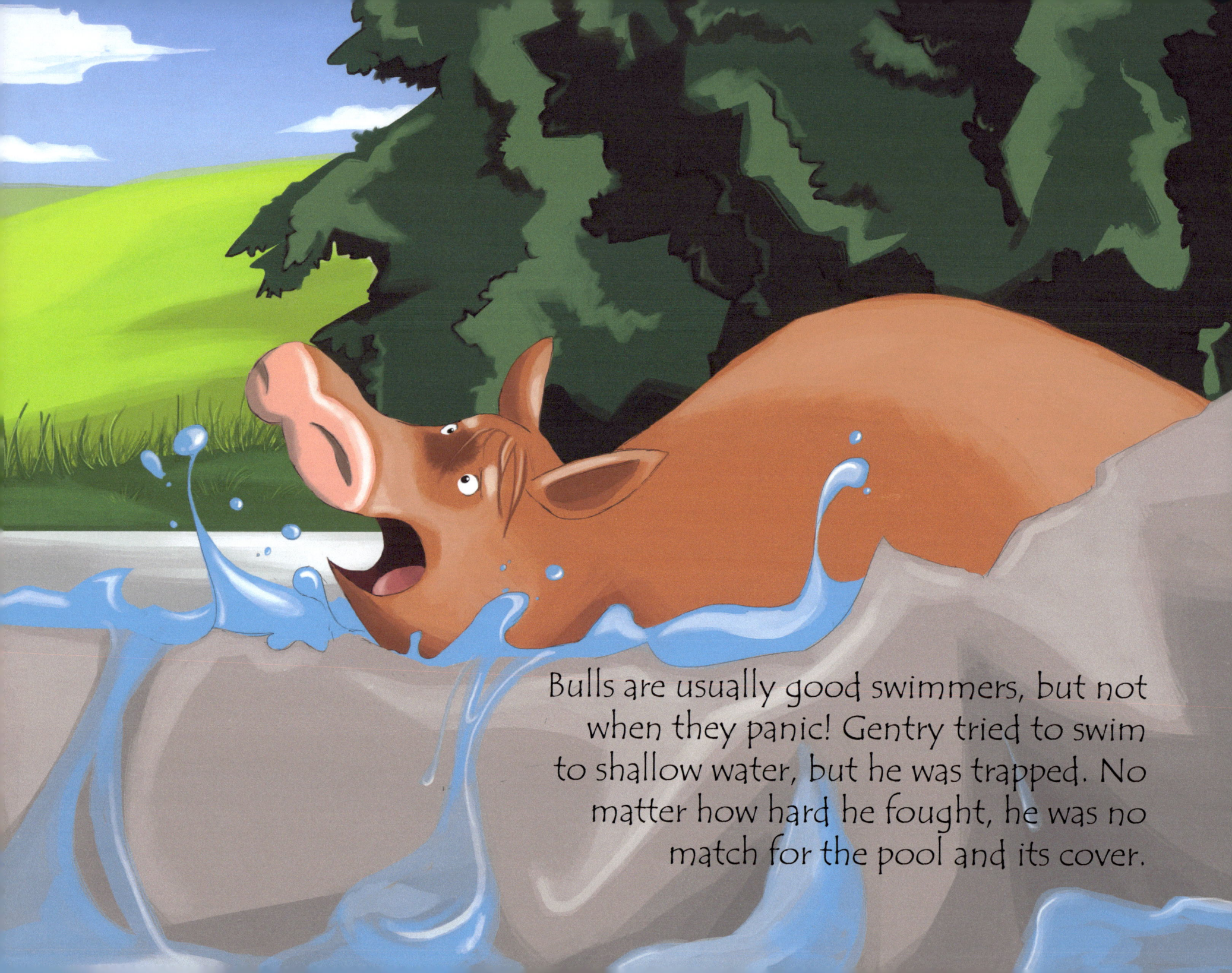

Bulls are usually good swimmers, but not when they panic! Gentry tried to swim to shallow water, but he was trapped. No matter how hard he fought, he was no match for the pool and its cover.

A watchful woman in the house looked down and saw Gentry struggling in the pool. Worried, the woman rushed out to the pool, scissors in hand, knowing there wasn't any time to lose!

In no time, the woman had cut enough of the cover to allow Gentry to swim safely to the shallow end. Gentry was no longer thinking about excitement and adventure. He felt both sad and scared. Rancher Dave was sure to be angry. After all, Gentry broke out of his fence and was now stuck in the neighbor's pool.

The worried woman sounded the alarm! Soon Rancher Dave and the whole town were there puzzling over the bull in the pool. Rancher Dave stood and frowned. Gentry felt terrible for running away and disappointing Rancher Dave.

All of the townspeople worked together to pull Gentry from the pool using Rancher Dave's big tractor and chains. The tractor slowly pulled Gentry's huge body up and away from the pool.

Everyone clapped and cheered!

Gentry was herded home and put back in his pen. He decided that was enough excitement and adventure for now. He was happy to be back home, safe in his pen and close to Rancher Dave. Gentry liked the smile on Rancher Dave's face. Maybe the ones we LOVE are more important than excitement and adventure?

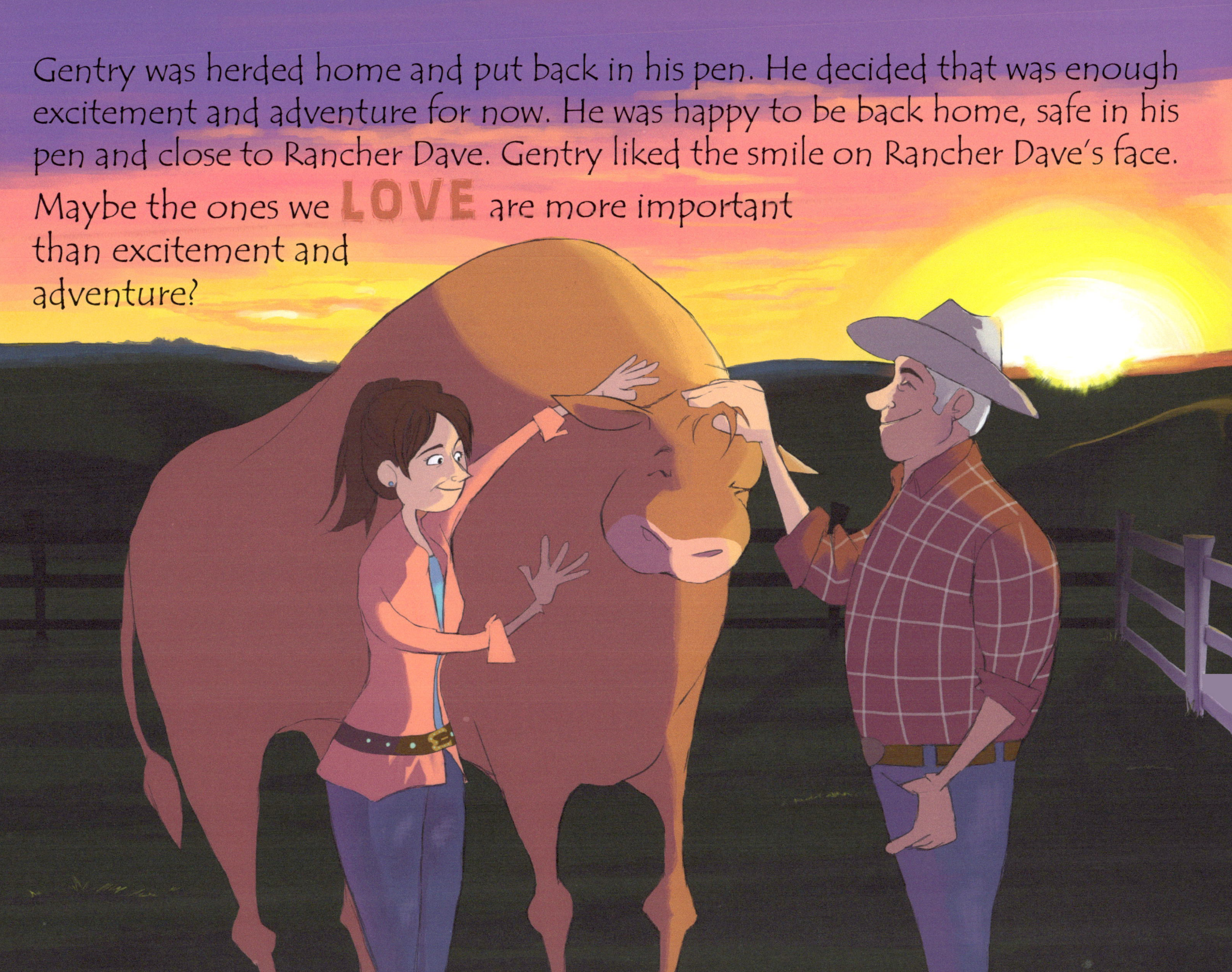

Word spread quickly through *the Heartland* about Rancher Dave's bull in the pool. The local news heard about Gentry and put him on television and in the newspaper.

Gentry, the runaway, swimming bull, was famous!

Today, people still come to see Gentry and to hear Rancher Dave's story of how his bull ended up in the neighbor's pool. The pool, now good as new, has a sign posted that reads, "No Bulls in Pool." If Gentry goes looking for adventure again, we already know he can swim…

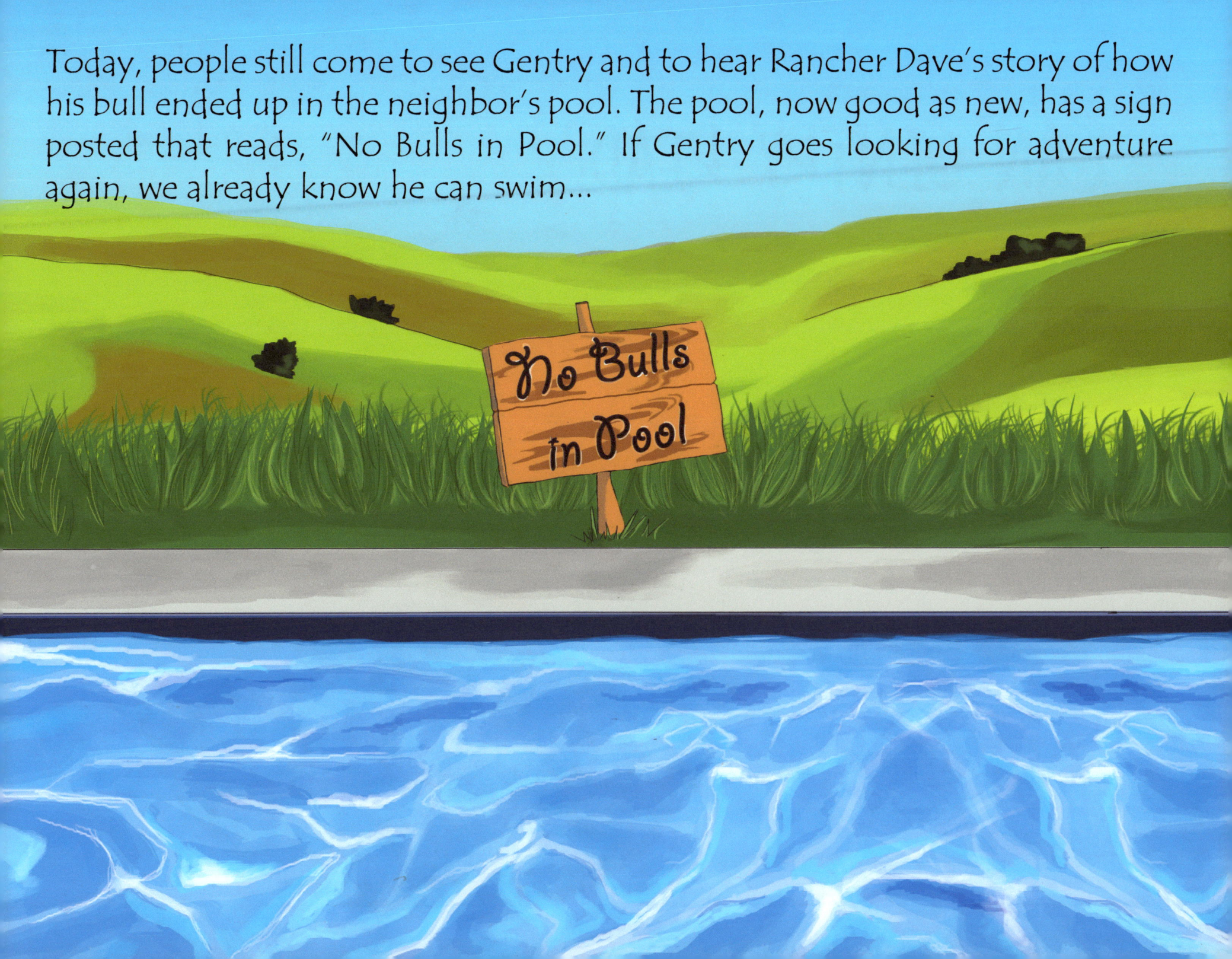

But, CAN GENTRY READ??

Rancher Dave and Gentry

Gentry in the pool!

www.ingramcontent.com/pod-product-compliance
Lightning Source LLC
Chambersburg PA
CBHW041457040426

42453CB00004B/124